soul poet

Paul B Allen III

Copyright © 2021 Paul B Allen III
All Rights Reserved

Soul Poet

No part of this book may be reproduced in any written, electronic, recording, or photocopying without written permission of the publisher or author. The exception would be in the case of brief quotations embodied in the critical Articles and review and pages where permission is specifically granted by the author Paul B Allen III.

Cover Portrait Photography: Paul B Allen IV
Front Cover Design: Paul B Allen III
Back Cover Design: Naeem Khan

Publisher: Paul B Allen III
City of Henderson, Nevada, USA
https://pba3.com/contact

Editor: Paul B Allen III
City of Henderson, Nevada, USA

Library of Congress Control Number: 2021902093

ISBN 978-1-7355721-3-0
1. Free Verse 2. Sonnets 3. Haiku 4. African American Poetry

First Edition
Printed in Henderson, Nevada, USA

10 9 8 7 6 5 4 3 2 1

soul poet

Contents

FREE VERSE	xi
King Étagère	*1*
Diamond, Silver, and Gold	*4*
What the Hell?	*6*
Pretty Stacks	*9*
In Moments like These	*11*
No Feet Deep	*13*
Life Is Never Fair	*15*
... Pants on Fire	*17*
No Mas	*20*
Jensen's	*22*
More Glorious	*27*
Sexy Substitute	*29*

Transporter *32*

Music to Her Ears *35*

Kiss like a Lunatic *37*

    SONNETS *39*

Doctor Mom *40*

Sweet Jekyll *41*

Saturn's Rings *42*

Quintessential Toast *43*

Wrestling with a Brat *44*

All *45*

Tainted Seed *46*

Seven Sisters *47*

Wanderlust *48*

Eyes That Sleep *49*

A Ship of Fools *50*

Dreams of Distant Times *51*

This Hero That I Never Knew *52*

The Greatest *53*

As I Have Loved No Other *54*

Never Just One Thing *55*

There's the Rub *56*

Romance at Work *57*

Muck Spout *58*

I'm Giving up on Women *59*

A Harder Row to Hoe *60*

Knowing You *61*

The Apple of My Eye *62*

Some Give, Some Take *63*

My Muse is Out of Town *64*

Tonight, You're Mine *65*

Not a Cat *66*

A Better Story *67*

Hikikomori *68*

The More Things Change *69*

A Southern Comfort Road Trip *70*

Ham for Jesus *71*

A Giant with a Name *72*

Just a Hamster on Their Wheel *73*

Only Fans *74*

The Leaves Do Not Believe *75*

LOVE POEMS 76
Sexy Visigoth *77*

My Queen Doth Rule No Kingdom 78

Captured by the Queen 79

A Life Newly Arisen 80

Questions 81

You Speak 83

Last Night 85

Peek-a-Boo 86

Mine 88

For Hearts to Beat in Sync 89

Siren Song 90

Noun, Noun, and a Verb 92

A Trip Around the Sun 93

Blue 94

Betwixt and Between 95

Counting Coup	*96*
intersect light	*97*
Dolemite	*98*
The Day We Met	*99*
`HAIKU`	101
Heroes	*104*
Remembering Glory	*105*
The Workout	*106*
3.0	*107*
Exploring Space	*108*
The Noble Expedition	*109*
Economics 101	*110*
Poetic Weather Forecaster	*111*
Yes, Waiter, Give Her the Check	*112*

Nowhere to Run *113*

Trying to Survive *114*

That's All, Folks! *115*

All That Glitters *116*

No Dice *117*

Birdland *118*

Luther Ingram *119*

Soprano to the Bass *120*

DEDICATIONS 122

About the Author *123*

FREE VERSE

King Étagère

I sit in an overstuffed chair,
as uncomfortable as I am oblivious,
staring at the spot where the TV lives no
longer.

Where, instead, King Étagère demands
exclusive devotion—and all my attention—as
he displays tchotchkes from days of old. They
are value-less yet valued beyond all fortunes.

On the top shelf live cats. They neither purr
nor beg to be let outside so that they can
lazily stretch in the warmth of the morning sun
or stalk and ambush their prey or engage in
prison breaks as they exercise their feline civil
disobedience and jump over the wall
into the neighbor's yard.

These are perfect pets, gifts from her adoring
eight-year-old son to his thin, anemic mother
who could use new kitten salt and pepper
shakers but had no time for living breathing
pets, not with her four young children bouncing
off Omaha walls like pinballs and devouring
every second of her time.

On the bottom shelf lies a pocket-sized

cigarette holder in green, a tin from the 1932
Chicago World's Fair. Grandfather purchased it
there the year that Father was born.

Had Grandpapa realized, perhaps even
prophesied? Was he an oracle or a Gypsy?

How else could he have known way back then
that his son would smoke five packs a day and
that cancer would take him away just one year
before it took Mom?

Could Grandsire also foresee how deeply I
would mourn?

Between bottom shelf and top of Monarch
Étagère sits an oval clock encased within a
crystal block: the perfect symbol, a gift from
their 48-year-old son who adored his parents
and wished to mark their lifetime of love and
commitment on their 50th wedding anniversary.

Even now that clock keeps perfect time—
twice a day.

Yet, in its silence, it speaks volumes.

The second hand protests, "I refuse to sweep."

With dispassionate calm, the Zen-like minute
hand admits, "I am always in the moment."

Relentlessly, the hour hand whispers, "Forever five."

And in this clock, time is locked and as still, and definite, as the memory of my parents. And, as I recall, I recall nothing before them.

For me, there is no happily ever—just grief and tears and intractable memories.

Like this broken clock, I cannot move—forward.

Diamond, Silver, and Gold

s I watch you sleep, it is I who dreams.

Lying there, most beautiful in my eyes, wrapped in innocence like swaddling, you remind me of a newborn babe, helpless, vulnerable, gorgeous, and loved beyond all comprehension.

I dream of the time we will celebrate our 10th wedding anniversary. Diamond jewelry, right? How silly of me to ask when I know positively.

And our 25th? I'm sorry, I can't help smiling. Something silver is the appropriate gift for that one, and you will have so earned it by that time.

Can you imagine putting up with my insanity for two-and-a-half decades? Only you could do it, and my silver gift will be but a small token of my immense appreciation.

And oh, the 50th, what a soiree we will have. We will pull out all the stops, and my gift of gold to you will stagger and amaze all who see it.

As I watch you sleep, it is I who dreams.

But the tears welling in my eyes replace my smile, knowing that my last gift to you was china and that you will never receive crystal or diamond or silver or gold, not according to the top specialists on either coast. Not according to the rattling cough that rips you from your dreams again tonight.

I hold you, tenderly comfort you, and lie to you as I whisper, "Everything is going to be fine."

What the Hell?

Once, I wore a pair of 3-D glasses. As I watched the movie, I was amazed, but was in no way prepared for what would happen when the glasses came off.

With credits rolling, I removed the glasses to find that my entire world was now in black and white.

As in, black and white, before there was color TV.

As in, as black and white as the pieces of a chessboard.

As in, piano keys are black and white.

I was at once fascinated and terrified.

What in the world is happening?
Will I ever see in living color again?

What the hell?

It took nearly half an hour, but soon everything was normal once more.

Apples were red. Oranges were orange.
Grapes were purple, black, red, or green.
The world was right again. What a relief!

Of course, I couldn't leave it at that.

*3-D glasses can't do that to you, can they?
It has to be something else*, I convinced
myself.

So, and I am sure my fellow nincompoops
would agree, I had to try it again.

And sure enough, I was right. After I took the
glasses off, there were no problems with the
loss of color. Not at all.

I could see all the colors of the rainbow—in
my right eye.

Ah, but the left eye. The left eye could see
only one color: black.

As in, black is the color of pitch.

As in, all I see is as black as tar.

As in, I could not see a shard of sunlight if I
were staring directly into the sun, kind of
black.

I was completely blind in that eye.

What in the world is happening?
Will my sight ever return?

What the hell?

After 45 minutes, I began to see
fuzzy shapes taking form in hues
of soft gray.

Not long after, the gray shapes became
more defined, and about an hour later I
could see clearly again and in color.

But 3-D glasses can't do that to you, can they?
It has to be something else, I convinced
myself.

Have you guessed what happened next? Well,
you'd probably be right, except that something
else happened first.

I told this story to my mother.

Unblinking, she looked deep into my eyes and
said, "Son, everybody is crazy—it's just to
what degree."

What the hell?

Pretty Stacks

They fill my living room. Magazines, everywhere I look, piled in stacks because there are so many of them.

They are purchased per annum and have been for years.

There is *Time*; *Entertainment Weekly*; *Psychology Today*; *Sports Illustrated*; *Better Homes and Gardens*; *Popular Mechanics*; *Wired*; and *Essence*.

There is *Rolling Stone*; *Art in America*; *Motor Trend*; *Variety*; *Vogue*; *Architectural Digest*; *GQ*; *Glamour*; *Travel and Leisure*; *Car and Driver*; *Rider*; and *Autoweek*.

There is *Wine Spectacular*; *Family Circle*; *Elle Décor*; *Digital Photo Pro*; *Elysian*; and *W*.

There are others as well.

Earlier this week, I caught the mailman giving me the finger when he thought I was not looking.

It made me wonder what his reaction would be if he knew the truth—that I never read any of them—that OCD grows tranquil amidst a sea of pretty stacks.

In Moments like These

as we lie on our deathbed and pray to
God, pleading with him to forgive us
our sins

as our girlfriend/boyfriend,
husband/wife/significant other
says, "we need to talk: this isn't
working out"

as the sheriff stands at the door
of our home to evict us

as our boss summons us to his office, tells us
to close the door and sit down,
then says that he has bad news

as someone demands that we hurry up

no matter where we are
who we are
what language we speak
the color of our skin
our political persuasion
our religious viewpoint
our sexual or social status

it is in moments like these that we prove
we are more alike than different as we
each make the same request:

"please, give me just a little more time."

No Feet Deep

I wish that I could write something deep.

Deep enough to make scholar's scratch
their heads, bewildered, confused,
frightened even. Frightened that someone had
written something that they know they could
never hope to understand in three lifetimes.

Something deeper than the Mariana Trench.
Deeper than deep space.
So deep that if you got to the bottom of it,
you would get the bends when you came back
up.

I wish I were profound and that my words
were proclaimed miraculous and enlightening.
I want to say something that will bring world
peace, inculcate racial equality, and end
starvation on this planet.

Can you imagine? No more war? ? No more
racial injustice? No more hunger?

Now that would be deep.

You must have a mind for such things,
but alas, I do not.

I am the tip of the tip of the iceberg.
I am the surface of the pool, no feet deep.
I am general conversation. "Great weather
we're having, isn't it?"
And if the discussion becomes any more
barometrically challenging than that,
I am out of there.

My nature desires what goes against my
nature.

I want what I cannot handle, and long for what
I could never attain.

Oh, wait a minute! I'm sorry, but the
commercials are over and

Bugs and Daffy are calling…

Life Is Never Fair

Oscar Wilde. The man could turn a phrase. "Life is never fair," he wrote, "and perhaps it is a good thing for most of us that it is not."

Every day I look at someone and hope they get what's coming to them.

Every day I wish I could point my finger and scream out loud, "I told you so," and though decorum dictates that I do not speak it, I am most certainly thinking it—with verve and glee—as I stifle a smile.

"Payback is a bitch," and "God don't like ugly," are two phrases of dispraise in the black community. They mean the same thing: I'll be glad when you get yours.

"What goes around comes around."
"You reap what you sow."
Even the word comeuppance has a beautiful ring to my ears—as long as it is not my comeuppance we are discussing.

And that is the point.

All the time we are thinking and wishing and hoping that someone else gets what they deserve, someone else is thinking and wishing and hoping the same thing about us.

"Life is never fair," wrote Mister Wilde, "and perhaps it is a good thing for most of us that it is not."

Of course, he could have just written, "A good mirror will kick your ass," but hey, that was Oscar.

... Pants on Fire

Have you ever wondered why?
Santa? The Tooth Fairy? The Easter Bunny?

When we are at the most vulnerable time in our lives, our parents delight in showering us with disinformation and prevarication. Simply put, they enjoy lying to us.

Don't they get how that will affect our development, and impact our future?

They don't bow their heads in shame or shiftily look from side to side as they do it.

Their statements don't come in mumbling, fragmented, hesitant clips because the words are just too hard for them to say as they look us in the eye.

No. With glee, our parents tell us tales about a jolly fat man who essentially runs a sweatshop at the North Pole (what irony?). They tell us that Little People are employed there who must work twenty-four hours a day, seven days a week, and never have a day off. And further, that they are purportedly happy about it. (Yes, at least as happy as was Kunta Kinte would be my educated guess.)

We hear about his reindeer, forced to pull his massively rotund frame all around the world in a single night, a feat from which they could not possibly recover until the next Christmas Eve.

Can't you hear a wheezing, pissed-off Rudolph talking to the other reindeer when they are just back in the stable after that Christmas night run?

"Damn... he's at least... a buck, buck and a quarter heavier than last year. I don't know how much more we can take. I'm going... I'm going to check into getting the union in here before next Christmas. He can bet his big fat lard ass on that one."

Our parents tell us about fiduciary agents who are tiny, winged, and philanthropic. They secretly hang out in the bedrooms of children, but only after the kids have fallen asleep. Oh, and did I mention that they also have a tooth fetish?

Well, they sound like my kind of people, all right.

The upside is that they pay well. I used to think about pulling out good teeth to make a little extra money because back in the day, you could buy a bagful of two-for-a-penny candy with only a quarter, but I digress.

And the Easter Bunny? Our folks, who will one day be upset when we fail biology class, purposely screw with our knowledge of biology by telling us the Easter Bunny lays eggs.

Lays eggs? Like a chicken or a duck or a bad comic?

Tell that to a rabbit who has just given live birth to 18 bunnies and see if you don't get cursed out big time.

So, thank you, folks, for teaching us that you revel in telling tall tales, and for showing us that when it comes to hard-line reporting, you just cannot be trusted.

All right. I'm going to catch up on the latest *National Enquirer* and check out a little news on *World Truth TV;* then I'm calling it a night.

No Mas

No more mortgage payments.
No more grocery bills.
No more exercise—that I never got
enough of anyway—because
I held it in complete disdain.

No more drama.
No more hurt feelings.
No more agreeing with someone
to keep the peace, even when
I know they are as wrong as wrong
can get.

No more arguments.
No more office politics to navigate.
No more apologizing for things
that were not my fault to begin with,
just because I hate sleeping alone on
a cold, lumpy couch.

No more worrying about if
I left the stove on in the house,
or if I locked the front door
upon my departure.

No more electric bills, heck,
no more utility bills whatsoever.
No more car payments (which seems
to be eternal, since the old car breaks

down on cue the day after the last payment
is made on the old contract).

And Hallelujah, hallelujah, hallelujah,
no more taxes, city, state, or federal!

I get it now, why death is celebrated
with a parade, music, and a party
in New Orleans.

These good folks may not grasp the adage,
"Location, location, location," but they
sure know what to do for you after
a person has breathed their last.

So glad I lived in New Orleans.

Jensen's

The corner store?
Dead as a doornail and as archaic
as that description.

Kaput. Done. Ghosted.
Say it how you will,
the corner store is history.

Walmart and Kmart and Target swallowed
them whole, devouring even their bones,
like a giant cyclops who recycles, leaving
nothing of its meal behind.

Now the neighborhood corner store exists only
in our memories of happier times—
the days of our youth—right
alongside memories of Santa, the Tooth Fairy,
and George Reeves as Superman.

And I do remember. I remember it all.

I remember Jensen's, in North Omaha.
It sat on the corner of Sprague and 25th
Avenue, only six or eight houses separating it
from my own, the last residence on a dead-end
street.

I remember that Mister Jensen, in appearance,
lived up to his Scandinavian surname. He was

tall and thin with wisps of blond hair
that in times past were no doubt
part of a mane of flowing golden locks.

The uniform he wore over his street clothes
was a long white apron that looped around his
neck and tied around his waist, and he wore it
as effortlessly as he wore his smile.

Amiable, affable, and amicable—
Mister Jensen was an A1 guy.

Mrs. Jensen was short and squat. She rarely
smiled, but when she did, it was genuine and
warm. She, too, wore a long white apron, just
like Mister Jensen's, but with her short, dark
hair, she did not appear to be Scandinavian in
the least.

They were Mutt and Jeff.

It was Jack Spratt with a pretty wife who was
not fat, but not so thin, and perhaps a decade
younger than her mister.

The jar that sat on the counter appeared huge
to my seven-year-old eyes. Humongous green
pickles floated in the brine. A nickel bought a
lip-puckering meal.

I remember that Jensen's extended credit. No paperwork required, not even a handshake requested. Just a note from my parents saying, "Please give Paulie this, this, and that, and we will pay you on Friday."

Mr. Jensen would fill a bag according to instructions, tuck the bill carefully inside it and hand it to me with a smile.

And always, Mr. Jensen was paid on Friday.

I believe he extended this same courtesy to every family in the neighborhood, and every family on the block was just the opposite of Scandinavian.

Mister and Missus Jensen were good-hearted folk, even when it came to money.

Jensen's carried caps for my pop gun.
Jensen's carried the Paddle Ball.
Jensen's carried Kraft Sandwich Spread, and an addictive substance that has killed millions more than heroin could on its best day.

I remember carrying a note from my parents to Mr. and Mrs. Jensen (I am beginning to wonder now if my mother and father ever set foot in the store), asking them to send me back home with a carton of cigarettes.

soul poet

I don't recall the brand or the price. But I do
remember giving Mr. Jensen the note and the
money and him giving me the tobacco.

I was a seven-year-old drug mule,
and not for the first time. Nor would
it be the last.

The late fifties and early sixties
were kinder, gentler, more trusting times.

There was no trash pick-up in those
days in that area. You burned your garbage
in 25-gallon barrels in your back yard. But
Jensen's was a business, so they had
a substantial furnace along the side of their
store that faced our street.

I remember my little sister being led home by
a group of older kids. She was holding her arm
and crying a cry I had never heard before and
have never heard the like of since.

Oh, yes, I have heard the screams of women in
labor, and they could not even come close to
the sound of pain I heard emanating from the
tiny lungs of my five-year-old baby sister.

Gayle had fallen off her bike up at the corner,
and her arm sizzled for far too long on the hot

furnace at Jensen's. Her third-degree burns
brought unimaginable pain, as did the series of
skin-graphs she had to endure afterward. For
the first time in my life, I knew the feeling of
frantic helplessness.

After that, the Jensen's put up a chain-linked
wire cage around that furnace so that no one
else would ever have to live through the
unlivable.

With such a terrible memory seared indelibly
into my mind—along with the Jensen's
colluding with my parents to turn me into a
drug mule—you would think that my feeling
towards Jensen's would be less than
magnanimous.

Not true. When I went back
to visit the old neighborhood, I learned that
Mr. and Mrs. Jensen had passed away—and so
had their corner store.

Now, all that was left was an empty lot
and the tears that welled in my eyes.

More Glorious

I bow to the knowledge you have gained through your battles with life.

You rose like a phoenix from the ashes each time unfavorable circumstance knocked you down, and you are still here to talk about it, never without a smile.

Your stories inspire me to be a better me than I was before you began your tale.

I listen

because your gray hair, diminishing stature, and failing eyesight tell me you were wise enough to survive longer than most of your contemporaries, and I wish to outlast most of mine.

I love you

in a different space, on a different level. I love my parents and children. But my love for you is expansive and all-inclusive and laced with equal parts of reverence and awe.

Perhaps it is because you loved me first and had visions of me decades before my parents became my parents.

I miss you

already. Even though you are here, I know you will not be with me for much longer. Today—any day—could be our final one together. You will leave and take with you the bridge that has forever connected me to my past.

But you will live, Grandsire, in my heart. And with your stories passed on to my progeny for generations to come,

you shall grow more glorious with each iteration.

Sexy Substitute

She was blond, blue-eyed, gorgeous, and shapely. She looked more like a Playboy model than a grade school teacher.

She said she was our substitute for the day.

From that moment on, to me, the word substitute meant the same thing as sexy.

But, lately, the word has lost some of its appeal.

I ordered strawberry preserves from the grocery store for home delivery but got strawberry spread instead. Same price (expensive), inferior quality, and content. Not a real strawberry to be found in the whole jar.

I ordered a dozen eggs and got eighteen in their place. More money and more eggs—that will go bad—because I can never eat that many eggs before the sell-by date.

I ordered four gallons of distilled water at 99 cents a gallon. However, my $4 charge evolved into a $16 tabulation. Why? A substitution that cost me an extra $3 per gallon.

Suddenly, the word substitute is no longer sexy, and I am seriously thinking of ending home grocery delivery in favor of going back into stores and picking the items myself.

Hmm… COVID. Shower, shave, style hair, add shirt and pants to my home uniform (my boxers). Warm up the car, drive to the store, then walk around there for the better part of an hour trying to locate what I need.

Face long checkout lines where I will invariably choose the wrong one—usually behind the lady who has a thousand coupons and pays $1.67 for two carts filled with groceries.

And to be sure, she will pay with exact change from her coin purse. There will be no folding money involved.

Next, I'll have to load the bags of groceries into my car, lug them from my trunk into my home, which will take several trips as I shop for a month at a time.

Then, already beat, I will have to put away everything I have just purchased.

Several hours of COVID exposure, walking, searching, lifting, and stretching. Geez, that sounds like a day spent at my least favorite spot in the world, the gym.

Okay, the word substitute is sexy again. Not as sexy as my fifth-grade substitute teacher, but you have to work with what you've got.

Transporter

The Time Tunnel
The Transporter on *Star Trek*
The Stargate on *Stargate*.

All mechanisms that could transport you
to different places, different times, and strange
new worlds.

I had one too when I was a child, my very
own Time Tunnel / Transporter / Stargate,
and I used it every day to escape the violent
streets I lived on in Omaha, Nebraska.

I was in search of adventure, new horizons,
with fresh—and very different—challenges to
overcome.

I transported to Cairo, Tokyo, London, Paris,
and Hong Kong.

King Arthur and Merlin the Magician were
my friends.

I walked the streets of Philadelphia
alongside a penniless Benjamin Franklin
before he became *Benjamin Franklin.*

In 1932, I stood near home plate at Wrigley
Field in Chicago and watched as the Great

Bambino, the Sultan of Swat, Babe Ruth
pointed to center field and then crushed a
home run to that exact spot. The crowd went
insane.

I was in the hidden room, with Anne Frank,
praying that the ruthless Nazis would not find
us and send us to Auschwitz, where we would
be starved to death or consigned to the gas
chambers or worse—have our bodies
experimented on while we were still alive—
and awake.

I stood with Captain Nemo and Captain Ahab.
I witnessed General Custer at his last stand.
I was as fast with a six-shooter as Billy the
Kid and as roguish and virtuous as Robin
Hood.

My Time Tunnel / Transporter / Stargate
could not have been less mechanical. But
one thing is for sure: it never lost its power
because Dilithium Crystals were running low.

Best of all, it fit into my pocket, and even as a
little boy, I could carry it with me everywhere
I went.

And I did.

Admittedly, it too had limitations, not the least of which was that it only worked when I stepped inside a library.

Still, without my library card, all there would have been was rhubarb, mulberries, crab apples, and me—growing wild in Omaha.

Music to Her Ears

When the mating call of a man
catches the ear of the female of the
species,

what does she hear?

Is it Luther Vandross singing a beautiful
love ballad, so light and intricate that she feels
the song is floating through air on gossamer
wings,

the lyrics so perfect that she knows this tune
was written about her

and sung for her alone?

Or does she instead hear the deep, sensual
urgings of Barry White,

with a vocal resonance
that makes her quiver deep inside?

Does she fall into a sensual stupor?

Does she tumble into that dark place
that she swore she would never
return to again, that place where passion and
madness steal control of her body and soul and
all her senses?

Or is it Sinatra she hears, with a big band
blowing hard behind him, hip and cool?

Does his perfect phrasing connect with her
intellect?

Do his words excite her psyche and take her
to faraway places that she has only dreamed of
but never thought she would see?

Do the prospects intrigue her?

Will she take yet another chance,
hoping this time that the mating call she hears
comes from Mr. Right?

Or in this mating call, does she hear the voice
of a father she never knew, but for whose
approval and warmth and love she has forever
longed?

Does his maturity, social status, and
willingness to protect her seem to be
everything that she has ever hoped for and
needed in her life?

When the mating call of a man catches the ear
of the female of the species,

what does she hear?

Kiss like a Lunatic

Why are you looking at me that way when you know what I say is true? You're an iconoclast, a firebrand, a muckraker, a malcontent. With you, the glass is always half-empty, never half-full.

We are opposing forces, and I have no idea how we ever came together or how we will stay that way.

Do opposites attract? Maybe it's true.

All I know is I will soon be bald, not because of alopecia or male pattern baldness, but because you are going to make me pull all my hair out as I try to cope with you and your shenanigans.

You have the IQ of Einstein, I know, but you are also as crazy as a bedbug.

On the other hand, you are damned cute, and you kiss like a lunatic. You know what I need, and you make sure I have it before I even know I want it.

You make me laugh until I cry. You make me stretch and grow. You spark within me the same sense of wonder I had as a child.

How can two people who are not on the same page, check that, not even in the same book, be such a perfect match?

There is but one certainty. From the second I met you, the world transformed, and so did I,

and I wouldn't change a thing.

SONNETS

Doctor Mom

Mercurochrome for little scrapes and cuts,
And castor oil (which constipation fights),
And ginger ale (to calm my gurgling guts),
Vick's VapoRub to ease congested nights.
And lemon juice she'd use when I was stung,
By any type of hornet, wasp, or bee.
She knew just what to do when I was young.
She had this home-spun style of alchemy.
A doctor's visit? Never heard of that.
An ambulance? That's only if you're dead.
Psychiatrist? Who's paying for that chat?
Prescription drugs? Are you out of your head?
Your potions and elixirs helped me through.
I'm still here, Doctor Mom, because of you.

Sweet Jekyll

My wife's the sweetest woman—heaven sent.
She sees the silver lining in all things.
She'll listen silently and let you vent.
Her smile will gift your troubled soul with wings.
My wife's the kindest woman I have known.
She'd sacrifice herself so you'd be fine.
And if this woman sat upon a throne,
We mortals would consider her divine.
I sense the hurricane makes landfall soon,
And Mount Vesuvius is 'bout to blow.
Here comes the *Creature from the Black Lagoon*,
And every pot and pan she's going to throw.
My angel keeps her devil locked inside,
But once a month, sweet Jekyll unlocks Hyde.

Saturn's Rings

I hear you, and my heartbeat picks up speed,
And I can smell the scent of your perfume.
An unkind word from you will make me bleed,
But three sweet words could save me from this gloom.
And when you laugh, I hear the world you're in,
And I can tell you're smiling when you speak.
The sound of your high heels tells me you're thin.
Your stride tells me you're confident, not weak.
I'd give the world if one time I could see,
The face that goes along with your sweet voice.
But I'm afraid that this will never be.
That's how it is, and I don't have a choice.
But in my mind, you look like Saturn's rings.
Each blind man who's in love sees different things.

Quintessential Toast

I have a soft spot for you, little heel;
One side of bread, one side a turtle's shell.
I can't imagine how that makes you feel.
I'm hoping that you take rejection well.
It's harder when you're unlike all the rest,
When you're ignored and smaller than they are.
Like them, you rose and passed each stringent test,
But live your life with one defining scar.
And they don't know you're quintessential toast;
That when it comes to texture, you stand tall.
You're confident and do not need to boast,
So they don't get that you protect them all.
Diversity is good, and with that said,
You heel, you are my fav'rite piece of bread.

Wrestling with a Brat

This problem with your feet, I've seen before.
It's getting worse each day? I understand.
Advice to see the doctor you deplore?
Let Grandpa share with you just what I've planned.
I know that this will cure your fungus foot.
The town will pee into a metal tub,
And when you stand inside of their output,
You're cured and now a member of the club!
But—everyone is here to help you out.
I know you'd never want to make them sad.
Come on and be a big boy, please, don't pout.
So now you think the doctor's not so bad?
There are more ways than one to skin a cat.
Call Grandpa when you're wrestling with a brat.

All

This month will be too long, I'm sad to say.
The cupboard is so bare it's nearly nude.
It's great to lose some weight, but not this way.
While some guys dream of girls, I dream of food.
The lights stay on for one more day or two.
The water's been turned off, good thing there's snow.
It's freezing coz the heater finally blew,
And I would leave, had I a place to go.
But I'm alive, and I still have my wits.
I have my health and strength, so there is hope.
I'm digging in; I'll never call it quits.
No matter what, I'll find a way to cope—
Like every other starving artist has,
Who gave their all for paint, or words, or jazz.

Tainted Seed

This tainted seed finds nourishment within the
the rains of terror—stress is making kids feel
like they're tortured on the rack

This poison seed is somehow nurtured
by the lack of sunshine. Their most important
person's gone, and they're not coming back.

Suicide's a virus as contagious as the rest,
but those who feel the loss the most are those
who hide it best.

Insidious, a killer, who's out to change their fate
and rarely is it treated as the signs are seen too
late.

Talk, listen, understand. Support them as they
grieve, that best friend that they ever had
who made the choice to leave.

A single tainted seed is sown that somehow
yields a cluster—

a seed of prickly decimation
deadly to the touch…

Seven Sisters

I know these seven sisters love to shine.
They give me hope that things are changing soon.
They're colorful. With curvature of spine,
They're mesmerizing as an August moon.
I love the way their names roll off my tongue
And dance through air to bring my ear delight.
Once they appear the song's already sung,
Now everything's about to be all right.
The faintest sister, Violet, appears.
Sweet Indigo then follows close behind,
As Blue and Green and Yellow calm all fears.
Are Orange and her sister Red aligned?
The rainbow swears a promise in the sky,
And these sweet seven sisters never lie.

Wanderlust

When walking unknown paths, I weary soon.
No matter if I've traveled near or far.
In time, it's like I'm stranded on the moon;
I miss my bed and long to drive my car.
No matter where I go, my heart stays here,
And in a foreign land or lost at sea,
The name of my hometown will catch my ear,
It feels like heaven sent a song to me.
But sometimes I just have to get away,
As cabin fever crucifies my soul.
I have to keep the boredom wolf at bay,
Or everything around me pays the toll.
There is no place like home, the place I trust,
But in my heart remains this wanderlust.

Eyes That Sleep

She's up all night and never will say why.
She listens to her music and zones out.
It moves her, and she laughs, but then she cries,
And I can only guess what it's about.
I think that she's afraid to close her eyes;
That nightmares from her past may haunt her dreams.
So, fighting sleep is now her way of life,
At least to me, that is the way it seems.
She's intellectual: sharp as a tack.
She's funny with a wit that's blinding: bright.
She moves ahead, and there's no looking back.
She's just this way as long as day has light.
Strange visions in the darkness can appear,
And eyes that sleep may open back in fear.

A Ship of Fools

We love it when the circus comes to town.
So many zany characters to see.
We know that they will never let us down.
Our dinner table will be filled with glee.
Thanksgiving brings them here most every time.
Shenanigans will start up right away.
And we both know there'll be some petty crime.
But everybody's feet are made of clay.
"In sickness and in health," we swore the words.
"For richer or for poorer," was our vow.
We know our relatives are loony birds,
But we're in love; let's just enjoy the chow.
We have such fun when family comes round.
It's like a ship of fools has run aground.

Dreams of Distant Times

There is this three-year-old I'm thinking of,
The cutest, sweetest thing you've ever seen.
It's certain she's a gift from high above,
This little earth-bound angel who's my queen.
There is this teenaged girl who's on my mind.
She's having fun with friends all over town,
Her teachers say her mind is very keen.
I can't recall I've ever seen her frown.
Then all at once, my baby disappears.
A woman stands where once there was a girl.
I must admit I can't fight back the tears.
My slumber has again caused time to swirl.
My mind unclouds in this, the break of day,
And dreams of distant times just fade away.

This Hero That I Never Knew

On the crowds, a gunman opens fire.
The theme park is as crowded as can be.
The news reports the situation's dire.
And shows the people as they hide or flee.
My heart is pounding wildly as I view
Each morbid detail passing on the screen.
My son is there right now; This can't be true!
Will he get out? He's only just a teen.
I'm told he did get out but raced back in,
To round up all his friends and save them too.
I must admit I've never been more proud
to meet this hero that I never knew.
We each are brave when danger's not around
When bullets fly is when a hero's found.

The Greatest

The greatest ballerina clearly fails.
Her pirouettes are always one turn shy.
Her plié sometimes goes right off the rails,
And others wonder why she'd even try.
The greatest female singer sings off-key.
That last note should be written off as loss.
But she insists that one day all will see,
She'll take the music scene just like a boss.
The greatest girl I know is going to win,
Yes, she whose talent pales beside her heart.
She rises when she falls and tries again,
And knows she's one step closer to her art.
One day I'm sure her story will be told.
Right now, the greatest star is six years old.

As I Have Loved No Other

As I have loved no other, I love you,
With feelings that I never knew I had.
Much deeper than the deepest shades of blue,
And more complex than any style of plaid.
The moment that I saw you, I was lost.
My soul was never captured in this way.
Your faintest smile makes my cold heart defrost,
And makes me buy you gifts with all my pay.
You son of daughter, whom I do adore.
My progeny, but somehow not the same.
My little lion who just loves to roar,
You share my blood and carry on my name.
I hold you in my arms with tears of joy,
On your first day as Grandpa's little boy.

Never Just One Thing

I think that love should come with warning signs,
Like "slippery when wet" or "curves ahead."
Instead, it comes with traps and hidden mines,
That blow and leave us hanging by a thread.
And love should be reviewed by C-D-C.
A virus that drives everyone insane?
This most contagious strain there'll ever be,
Can make us wander naked in the rain.
Love lifts us up and never will it fail.
Love conquers all and gives the hopeless hope.
Love is a ship that makes our hearts set sail,
And in this crazy world, it helps us cope.
What we call love is never just one thing.
To each of us, love brings what it will bring.

There's the Rub

I know a woman with a gorgeous mind.
Each time we speak, it's like we're on a date.
She's brilliant and so funny that I find,
I hunger for her words: I just can't wait!
I also know that she is very bold;
An astronaut who's going up in space.
Her smile is always warm, or so I'm told.
In court today, she's arguing a case.
Behind closed doors, she says she's truly bad,
As sinful, and as sexy as can be.
With face and body that would drive me mad,
If face and body, I could ever see.
To find romance online, just join a club.
With whom we are in love, now there's the rub.

Romance at Work

At work, a firecracker just walked in.
She stops me in my tracks with smoky eyes.
She smiles at me; I get this stupid grin,
As if I had just won the Noble Prize.
I blinked, and then the next thing that I knew,
We fell in love, and we fell hard and deep.
Wildfires in the wind; how our love grew.
I dreamed of her each day and in my sleep.
Now she walks in, and all I feel is heat,
And you could cut the tension with a knife.
Her look tells me that soon I'll be dead meat.
The love is gone, and now there's only strife.
Romance at work is never hard to find,
But someone's going to lose their job—or mind.

Muck Spout

You are a total muck-spout, yes, you are,
And "Potty-Mouth" should be your middle name.
With such a tongue, we two won't get too far;
I don't like girls who play the cursing game.
And you're a busy body, yes, it's true.
When others hurt, you're feeding on their pain.
You guzzle down their anguish like it's brew;
Since you've come 'round, I'm circling the drain.
 What happened to the cool girl? Where'd she go?
That "live and let live" you, so filled with Zen.
Or was that just the first act of your show,
To drag my carcass deep inside your den?
 I see it makes no sense to pay this freight.
 I've never had so bad a second date.

I'm Giving up on Women

I'm giving up on women, don't you know?
They simply are impossible to please.
There is no happy ending to that show.
And all their drama makes my poor heart seize.
I'm giving up on dating them as well.
They change directions like a weathervane.
They could say, "No," instead the lies they tell!
Just one more date, and I'll end up insane.
But they're so pretty, and it's such a fight,
To keep my distance and appear nonplussed.
When holding them and kissing them feels right,
I just can't figure out which head to trust.
I'm giving up on women, dare I say?
I'm starting very soon, just not today.

A Harder Row to Hoe

I can't explain exactly why I do.
You're polarizing, just to say the least.
I have this feeling I believe is true.
Your mind is never folded, stacked, or creased.
So why am I attracted in this way?
What makes me want to gamble all my chips?
What makes me hope that you'll come out and play,
With ire and with ever-pouting lips?
Some girls would make life easy, yes, it's true.
No pressure and no heat, I say, "No go."
A simple girl for me will never do.
Some men just need a harder row to hoe.
I want a girl whose drama makes the news,
Whose crazy sometimes makes me sing the blues.

Knowing You

Is it the magnetism of the moon,
That's pulling us as close as hand in glove?
Or is it that we're in the month of June,
That makes me feel the power of your love?
Or did a four-leaf clover make it so?
When sailing, did I hear your siren's song?
Or did I find romance within your glow,
That captured me, no matter right or wrong?
It couldn't be the timbre of your voice.
It couldn't be that freckle on your chin.
It couldn't be your gorgeous leaves no choice,
Or when you're caught you flash that sexy grin.
No, not the moon, or month, nor your warm glow,
It's knowing you that makes me love you so.

The Apple of My Eye

Astounded and amazed is what I am.
I'm happy for the first time in my life.
I'm eating home-cooked meals that have no SPAM,
Prepared with loving hands by my new wife.
She's pretty, and she's sexy, that's a fact.
But in the kitchen, she's a world-class chef.
I'm doing all I can to not get sacked,
And stay the bass to her sweet treble clef.
I bid a fond adieu to eggs and SPAM,
And Frosted Flakes and Wheat Chex fare-thee-well.
And "Oh, how do you do," to steak and lamb.
This angel saved me from my fast-food hell.
My woman is the apple of my eye,
But hated by my former pizza guy.

Some Give, Some Take

My ham and eggs are perfectly prepared.
This feast of love was made with care and zeal.
The toasted sourdough with jam is paired,
And fried potatoes still retain their peel.
The orange juice sits in a frosted glass.
The coffee's hot, three sugars, black, no cream.
A bacon rash and beans; some U.K. class.
The pancakes look as if they're from a dream.
But I'm afraid I'm not a breakfast guy.
I'm thin and rarely eat before it's noon.
Still, I dig in; don't want to make her cry,
Or this could be the shortest honeymoon.
They say that marriage is some give, some take.
I only pray to God she doesn't bake.

My Muse is Out of Town

My muse is out of town; I don't know where.
I don't know why she'd leave me all alone.
She pogo-sticked or hopped a train somewhere.
Without her, I'm afraid my cover's blown.
My inspiration's somehow fallen flat.
I'm staring at a page that has no words.
I hope she makes it back in time to chat.
My thoughts come now as stragglers, not in herds.
She took with her my glibness and my wit.
She took with her my focus and my thoughts.
And in her tiny purse, they seemed to fit,
With room for all the other stuff I've lost.
Without my muse, my words don't dance or sing.
But when she's near, my words are fresh as spring.

Tonight, You're Mine

I stroke your body with this lucky hand.
I open you and breathe you deep inside.
I run my fingers down your spine and plan,
To cede control and let you be my guide.
And nights like these are growing all too rare.
Seems, lately, we have spent so little time.
Don't get me wrong or think that I don't care;
When we are not as one, it's like a crime.
You look so hot bound in your leather dress,
That touching you gives me a tantric thrill.
And using just your words, I must confess,
You mesmerize and bend me to your will.
A science-fiction tale will work just fine.
My eyes will drink your words: tonight, you're mine.

Not a Cat

The single plant I have fights for its life.
Each day I see it reaching for the sun.
I know it wishes that I had a wife.
It fears that one day soon, it will be done.
It was a gift from a dear friend of mine.
What she was thinking, I just couldn't tell.
I always thought she thought that I was fine.
I guess she thinks that plant-less isn't swell.
I water, and I watch it as it grows.
If it takes more, it surely won't survive.
And caring for it keeps me on my toes.
But we both know that it will never thrive.
The next time that my friend comes here to chat,
She'll be so glad her gift was not a cat.

soul poet

A Better Story

I'm leaving here, and there's no looking back.
Once paradise is lost, there's only pain.
Our train derailed somewhere along the track.
Once paradise is lost, what's there to gain?
It's time I go, no need for mincing words.
You cheated, and you lied, but you don't care.
This current situation's for the birds.
There's nothing left to give or grin and bear.
You have my resignation as of now.
You'll never find another one like me.
But get some other horse to pull your plow,
I'll lose the shirt and tie, and I'll be free.
Some other fool can claim your watch of gold,
I'll live a better story, to be told.

Hikikomori

Sometimes I feel like I am lost in space,
Or walking through some kind of twilight zone.
It's like I've lost before I start the race.
I hide out like a spy whose cover's blown.
I'm not like other people, this I know.
My type of personality is rare.
If everyone is summer, I am snow.
To every round hole, I am just a square.
But is it strange to like to be alone?
I find my company is not so bad.
And is it strange to hate the mobile phone?
Intrusions in my life just make me sad.
If others feel like me, I wonder though?
I don't leave home, so I will never know.

The More Things Change

If prehistoric man were here today,
 He'd be surprised how many things have changed.
We drive, we fly, we're sailing in the bay;
He'd doubt his eyes and think he was deranged.
It's time to hunt? My friend, forget your spear.
A store has all you need; you'll be just fine.
Pick out a porterhouse and grab a beer,
And for your girl, a bottle of sweet wine.
But some things have not changed; he'd quickly see
That men treat women just like in his day;
That every leader claims he's got the key;
And each religion claims to be the way.
In minutes he would recognize our game.
The more things change, the more they stay the same.

A Southern Comfort Road Trip

A Texas Whataburger? I can't wait.
Louisiana gumbo? Be there soon!
Hey, Mississippi soul food—it's a date.
You, Alabama pulled pork, make me swoon.
Now, Florida, I need your key lime pie,
And Brunswick stew in Georgia, you're my thrill.
For Carolina's barbecue, I'd die,
But for Virginia's blue crabs, I would kill.
Like sweet potato fries in Tennessee,
Kentucky hot browns make my taste buds shout.
And I'm as close to heaven as can be,
As Arkansas' fried catfish turns me out.
Mint juleps, Dr Pepper, and sweet tea —
A southern comfort road trip's calling me!

Ham for Jesus

We love a chance our family to see.
We gather and have fun; our faces shine.
To share this time a holiday's the key.
We'll have a meal and maybe drink some wine.
Like lemmings over cliffs headlong we go.
We do so many things and just don't think.
And we are slaves of custom's little show,
With even food we eat and drinks we drink.
For Easter, baking ham's the standard call.
But eating pork is not the Jewish way.
A ham for Jesus makes no sense at all.
Could lamb or tofu be a better play?
I'm not a sheep: no gun held to my head.
I choose to lead instead of being led.

A Giant with a Name

Some icons of the past now grace my wall.
Musicians, every one, cause that's my game.
In stature, some were short, and some were tall,
But each one was a giant with a name.
Ma Rainey, Bessie Smith, and Lady Day.
Thelonious, and Miles, and Cannonball.
James Brown, and Bluey, Wayne, and Augie J,
No matter where I move, I take them all.
Your images inspire me no end.
When stuck, I ask, "How would you handle it?"
And each of you has now become a friend.
Your voices faint still urge me, "Never quit."
I look at you and listen every day.
And I thank God for you who paved the way.

Just a Hamster on Their Wheel

I want to hop inside my car and drive,
To gaze upon the many things I've missed.
This bee must leave the honey and the hive,
And start to live instead of just exist.
Coz working for another takes some Zen.
I've toiled just like a mule is how I feel.
I've given time to enrich other men.
But I am just a hamster on their wheel.
I'm going to drive until my mind is clear.
This break is just exactly what I need.
I'll hit some dives and drown my past in beer,
Come back and start a new life and succeed.
I'm glad I've taken stock, it's time I grew,
And left behind the old me for the new.

Only Fans

When we were children, everyone read books.
The library was deemed a sacred place.
And no one gave you dirty looks as you,
Escaped your mortal coil, without a trace.
Do you remember sitting there in peace,
For hours lost in space or lost at sea?
Or visiting the Parthenon in Greece,
Or tasting your first cup of Chinese tea?
The paradigm has shifted; things have changed.
We're force-fed dreams of others on the screen.
From our imaginations, we're estranged.
For poor Gen Alpha, what's this going to mean?
If we don't put more books into their hands,
Our kids won't be creators, only fans.

The Leaves Do Not Believe

The maple tree is filled with buds anew,
And all the possibilities life brings,
As Mother Nature's belly gives birth to
The verdant blades of carpet fit for kings.
And with the warmth of Heaven's golden eye,
The buds turn into leaves that thrive and grow.
The leaves do not believe they'll ever die.
What's moving fast they feel is moving slow.
What once was green takes on a reddish glow.
When beauty comes their power does decline.
Then one by one, each hanging leaf lets go,
Until the day that none are left behind.
No matter great or small the shadow cast,
Each leaf becomes a mem'ry of the past.

Paul B Allen III

LOVE POEMS

Sexy Visigoth

Like the mountain brings Muhammad
Like the bright flame brings the moth
Like the North Star brings the traveler
Like the chicken brings the broth
You speak in three-word phrases
That bring my heart to you
I don't know how you do it
But I marvel when you do

You confided *I adore you*
And our universe took form
I love Scotland you next stated
And our future plan was born.
You told me, *I'm beside you*
And I knew it for a fact
That I was born to love you and
There'd be no looking back.

Like Muhammad destroyed Frazier
Like the bright flame burns the moth
Your three-word phrases slay me
You sexy Visigoth

My Queen Doth Rule No Kingdom

My queen doth rule no kingdom
    No ocean nor a sea
    The wind doth not bow down to her
And no one bends the knee
She hath one lowly servant
And for her I would die
I'll slay the errant dragon
Who would dare to make her cry
She is my sun and starlight
I ne'er long to be free
My queen doth rule no kingdom
But rules the heart of me.

Captured by the Queen

I do not know what happens
I cannot tell you true
But setting foot in Kansas
Could spell the end of you.

She doesn't own a broomstick
Won't frighten you with "Boo!"
She doesn't have to see or touch
To cast her spell on you.

Your heart will really start to pound
Your ears will hear a ringing sound
Your buckling knees will put you down
No more you will be seen

You have been had, and had real good
She springs the trap I warned she would
Her chess-like moves misunderstood
You're captured by the Queen.

A Life Newly Arisen

You hit me with your love so hard
I think I may need traction
Your love-bug bite just kicks my ass
But brings me satisfaction.

You drop a ton of bricks on me
Then drug me with desire
You knock me down and blow me up
But then you lift me higher.

You throw me in the deep end and
Proceed to sink or swim me
You dried the wood and struck the match
And rekindled the chimney

What shall I do to so bad you
Who slaps me in Love Prison
Kiss your sweet lips and thank you for
A life newly arisen

Questions

I always take for Gospel
   Those words tumbling from your mouth
   As you share with me the happenings
From North, East, West, and South

We talk about minutia
And then the universe
We talk when going forward
And we talk while in reverse

Sometimes we speak in English
With words that never stall
Some days we talk forever
Some cursed days not at all

And yet I have some questions
That may take you by surprise
Like what day is your birthday
And what color are your eyes

Will you moan when first I kiss you
Will you grow weak in the knees
Are you an easy lover
Or granite hard to please

Will I find that you are ticklish
That your sneeze may make you pee

But only just a little
(Your secret's safe with me)

Do you like my little poems
Do they start your morning right
How sleep-deprived will we be
As we laugh and love all night

You Speak

My fantasies
of you abound
From you
there is
no mundane sound
That little voice
I cherish so
Sends me to worlds
I did not know

I learn
I grow
I morph
I change

My song
no longer
seems so strange
Till you
I was
misunderstood
I always thought
I always would

A solace
a salve
a balm
a cure

Your little voice
makes love
so pure.

My Afro
my Anglo,
my genius,
my Greek

You change my world
every time that
you speak

Last Night

I learned something last night
That took me by surprise
Put a lump here my throat
And it misted up my eyes

It threw me for a loop
Had me waiting for asides
You proved that dreams come true
That your shake comes with your fries

You showed me hidden feelings
Mariana Trench-like deep
You opened up your heart
And I saw me in its keep

I learned how dear you hold me
Even though I'm not in sight
I'm with you every second
That is what I learned last night

Peek-a-Boo

Peek-a-boo!

I see you, Little Boots
As you walk around the farm
And you lead your little troops—
As you lift your little arms
And grandma strips you bare
And throws you in the bathtub
And ponytails your hair.

Peek-a-boo!

I see you, Little Boots,
With wigglies in your pockets
Making Grandma gray her roots.
And when they thought they lost you
Is when you found they cared
And that is when your world changed
And life became more fair.

Peek-a-boo!

I see you, Little Boots.
A multitude of cultures
Yields your multitude of truths.

soul poet

Though one day you will grow up
And forget the games you knew,
I won't forget that little girl
Who giggled, "Peek-a-boo."

Mine

My Noodle
My Baby
My Savior
My Lady
My Best Friend
My Monsoon
My Comic
My Full Moon
My North Star
My Dreamer
My Coffee
My Creamer
My Red Queen
Of Fashion
Forever My
Passion

For Hearts to Beat in Sync

Your laugh alone enraptures me
And quells the harsh cacophony
That pokes and prods and tortures me
And takes me to the brink

Your eyes that smolder capture me
Your groovy is my symphony
Come play, perform, and always be
My breath, my food, my drink.

Your love I'll never push away
Through roughest night and darkest day
I'll scrape and fight to find a way
For hearts to beat in sync

Siren Song

From the gap
   when you sing "L_ve"
    To the gap
between your thighs

From your long
and slender fingers
To your changing
colored eyes

From your hips
that give you swivel
To your lips
I long to kiss

From your long legs
that excite me
And the hair
you sometimes flip

From that
little voice
that moves me
Guaranteed to turn me on

I crave you
Little A+

soul poet

And I hear your
siren song.

Noun, Noun, and a Verb

Sugar walls?
How inviting.
Girl who shines?
So exciting.

I'm in love with you
Noun, noun, and a verb

Tubs and spouts?
How arousing.
Moans and shouts?
Mesmerizing.

I can't live without
Noun, noun, and a verb.

A Trip Around the Sun

I must congratulate you
On another year well done

Accomplishments aplenty
And you've only just begun

Expanding your horizons
With a reach beyond your grasp

Achieving things stupendous
Despite trials that plagued your past

This year has been my best year
So much laughter—so much fun

I fell in love beside you
On your trip around the sun.

Blue

When my Baby cries
It makes the angels weep
And all the strong grow weary
And even lions peep.

When my Baby cries
Her tears are shards of glass
That rip away my heart
As I scrutinize my past

When my Baby cries
Life changes up the view
And through its misty lens
all colors change to blue.

Betwixt and Between

For the taste of you
I would give
a king's ransom,

the lion's share,

the motherload.

I want the tittle and jot of you
to the whole lot of you

and all that's betwixt and between.

Counting Coup

I love my little Noodle
  Who is known by many names
  She laughs cajoles and teases me
And thrills to our love games

To others she is quiet
And she rarely makes a fuss
But put her on a phone with me
It's seven hours plus

Her love is quite outstanding
Though her words can't verify
But let a barker come at me
Reactions never lie

I love my little Noodle
A warrior—a girl
Who counted coup and captured me
Her weapon is her swirl

intersect light

i met this woman
with walls divine
i met her humor
fell for her mind

only this shimmer
can shimmer me right
because we're magnetic
we intersect light.

Dolemite

I sing to you and you to me
creating brand new harmony
A groovy pure and sweet refrain
uniquely for us two

The world has never seen the like
We love to love and loathe to fight
We even both like Dolemite?
I'm so in love with you.

The Day We Met

The day we met
   The world began
   In retrospect
So says this man

You move me from
My head to toe
And make me come
When I should go
You make me strive
When I would quit
Inspire me
To be more fit

The world began
The day we met
So says this man
In retrospect

And you became
My drug of choice
With cravings for
Your little voice
You make me laugh
When I should cry
And fight to live
Instead of die

In retrospect
So says this man
The day we met
The world began

My conscious thoughts
And fantasies
My days and nights
And all my dreams
And all that I
Aspire to
Is not for me
But all for you

So says this man
In retrospect
The world began
The day we met

soul poet

HAIKU

Different Smokes for Different Folks

She smokes cannabis
he smokes turkey—they both sleep
very well each night

Heroes

the lone ranger and
batman and spider-man too
my heroes wear masks

Remembering Glory

Air-bound leaves recall
glory days as children toss
them into the wind

The Workout

**the warm morning sun
feline yoga. cat stretches—
then falls back asleep**

3.0

**Run jump skip flip roll
Grandson—reminding me that
we live forever**

Exploring Space

**Navigating aisles
a Magellan afternoon
Which book to read next?**

The Noble Expedition

snail travels inches
man travels the globe—find the
wonder in all things

Economics 101

**the world is a loo
so now toilet tissue is?
right! same price as gold**

Poetic Weather Forecaster

**a million-billion
pieces of heavenly art!
smile—snow falls tonight**

Yes, Waiter, Give Her the Check

Believe in Santa?
Check. And the Tooth Fairy? Check
COVID? No check, huh?

Nowhere to Run

mirror shows my face
bookcase displays my soul, and
nothing is concealed

Trying to Survive

a drop of water
gravity pulling from spout
like me, hanging on

That's All, Folks!

life: the bottom line?
from bud to leaf to compost.
any more questions?

All That Glitters…

a sparkling pot that
is dirty on the inside—
hypocrite defined

No Dice

**squirrel hiding nuts—
uncertain of the future,
taking no chances**

Birdland

**Orioles, Penguins,
Ravens. Those birds really sang.
Fifties vocal groups.**

Luther Ingram

Cookies, pies, and cakes—
"If loving you is wrong, I
don't want to be right."

Soprano to the Bass

**leaves stretching for sun
roots diving deep for water
life is harmony**

THE END

soul poet

DEDICATIONS

This book is dedicated to my son, Paul B Allen IV and my daughter Brooke Shalimar Allen-Rodrigues and my grandson, Zane Elijah Waller. You three are my pride and joy, and you make my life worth living.

I also dedicate this book to the Red Queen of Kansas, who is always there when I need a reason to smile…

Thank you:

Paul B Allen IV: Cover Portrait Photograph
Adam Bouse: Cover Seascape Photograph
Hannah Tims: Free Verse Photograph
Bernadette Gatsby: Sonnet Photograph
Nick Fewings: Love Poems Photograph
James Pond: Haiku Photograph
Naeem Khan: Back Cover Design

About the Author

Paul B Allen III has been a professional singer/songwriter for nearly fifty years. His best-known songs are "Always There" (Recorded by the UK group Incognito and the American group Side Effect), and "Such A Good Feeling" recorded by Brothers In Rhythm.

"Such A Good Feeling" is one of the "Greatest 100 Dance Singles of All Time" according to the venerable dance music magazine *Mixmag*.

Allen has also served as the lead vocalist of a legendary vocal group, The Platters ("Only You" "Smoke Gets in Your Eyes" and "The Great Pretender"). As such, he has led the group performances at prestigious venues worldwide, including the Kennedy Center.

He has performed for the Royal Family in England, for Prince Albert of Monaco, and the President and First Lady of Fiji. Shortly after the Monaco performances, Allen received an invitation to perform for the President of the United States of America.

Eclectic is the word that best describes Allen's style of writing. *Soul Poet* is his seventh book to date. The other six are:

The Saturday Mornings Song Chronicles: Memoirs, Motown, and Music – biographies of R&B musical icons and personal stories of the author's interactions with many of them, both as an internationally published hit songwriter and as the lead vocalist of The Platters. This book was recently named one of the "32 Best R&B Music Books Of All Time" by BookAuthority.

Benjamin Franklin: Time Tripper - A historical science fiction/fantasy that finds Benjamin Franklin transported to the Haight/Ashbury district of San Francisco in the mid-1960s.

Urban Haiku – East meets West. Traditional haiku structure populated with lyrical urban sensibilities.

The Tall Tales of Obadiah Short - Whimsical short stories told by a man who claims that he is "the oldest human in the history of the world."

The Power of X - A female anti-hero science fiction story that takes place on Earth 2, written as a screenplay.

From Karaoke to The Platters - An autobiographical "how-to" book that focuses on breaking into the music industry following the step-by-step method used and recorded by the author.

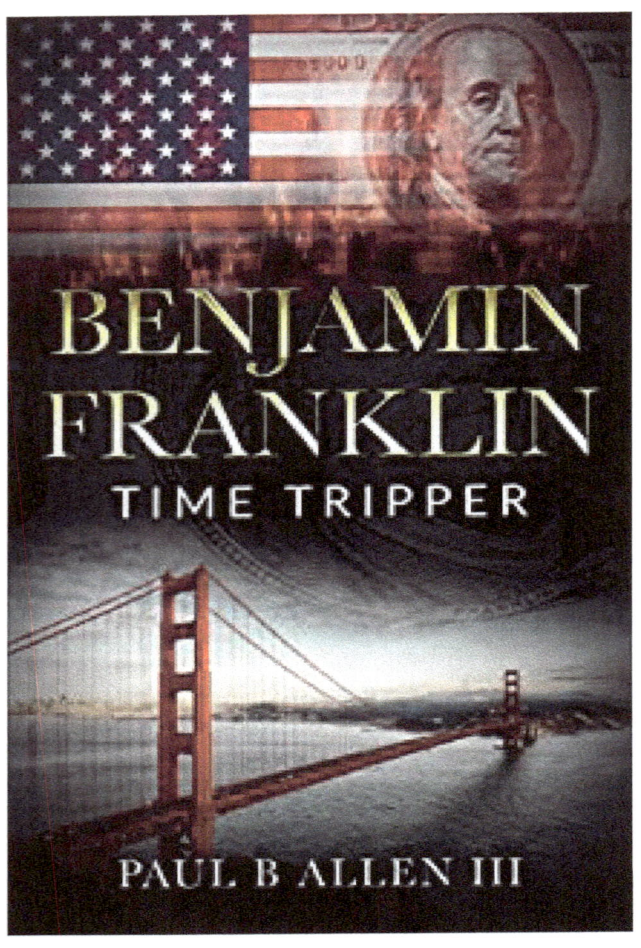

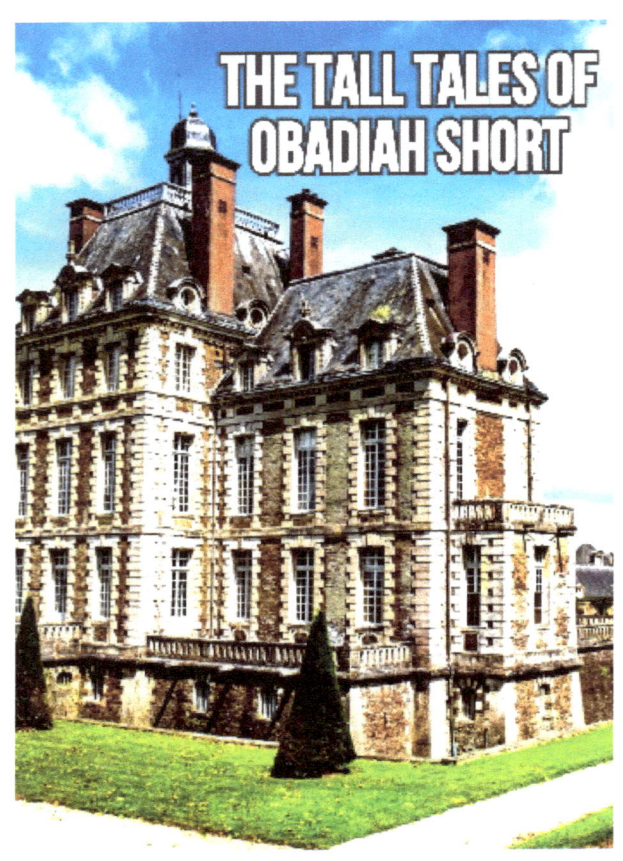

www.ingramcontent.com/pod-product-compliance
Lightning Source LLC
Chambersburg PA
CBHW040638100526
44583CB00038B/3059